LEST WE FORGET The Triumph Over Slavery

The Schomburg Center for Research in Black Culture • The New York Public Library

Pomegranate

SAN FRANCISCO

D1127994

Pomegranate Communications, Inc.
Box 808022, Petaluma CA 94975
800 227 1428; www.pomegranate.com

Pomegranate Europe Ltd.
Unit 1, Heathcote Business Centre, Hurlbutt Road
Warwick, Warwickshire CV34 6TD, UK
[+44] 0 1926 430111; sales@pomeurope.co.uk

ISBN 978-0-7649-4037-8

Pomegranate Catalog No. AA377

Pomegranate publishes books of postcards on a wide range of subjects.
Please contact the publisher for more information.

Cover designed by Shannon Lemme
Printed in Korea
16 15 14 13 12 11 10   10 9 8 7 6 5 4 3 2

To facilitate detachment of the postcards from this book, fold each card along its perforation line before tearing.

Much has been written about the transatlantic slave trade and slavery in the Americas. Unfortunately, most of the commentary on the human dimension of slavery has focused on the treatment of enslaved Africans—the trauma of capture and enslavement, the horrors of the middle passage, the grueling and at times dehumanizing regime of plantation work, the unwarranted cruelty and brutality of the slavery systems established in the Americas.

Slavery was vicious, brutal, and dehumanizing. And so, the focus on black victimization is certainly warranted. But, to paraphrase Ralph Ellison, slavery was not simply the sum total of black victimization. In the midst of slavery with all its oppressiveness, in the midst of the process of dehumanization, which was intended to make conscious, critically thinking, enslaved African human beings comply with the demands of the enslavers, an extraordinarily human and humanizing process was being authored and lived out by the enslaved Africans. New languages and new religions were being invented and practiced. New art forms and new music and dances were being created. New forms of family life and social organizations were being experimented with and put into practice. In short, new world Africans were creating and re-creating themselves anew in the midst of slavery.

Those who managed to gain their freedom during and after the slavery era used these new world African social and cultural resources to continue to create new institutions, organizations, and forms of human expression and existence. The foundations of African American economic, political, social, and cultural life can be traced to the struggles waged by enslaved and free Africans during slavery.

Howard Dodson
Schomburg Center Director

LEST WE FORGET
The Triumph Over Slavery

Water Passage

Oil on canvas, 1990

Artist: Rod Brown

Private collection of Ms. Velma May

BOX 808022 PETALUMA CA 94975

Pomegranate

Sung with Great Success by Alma Gluck

Carry me Back to Old Virginny

Song and Chorus

by

James A. Bland

50

Boston-Oliver Ditson Company

New York-Chas. H. Ditson & Co. ♫ ♫ ♫ Chicago-Lyon & Healy

LEST WE FORGET
The Triumph Over Slavery

"Carry Me Back to Old Virginny"

Sheet music cover, c. 1878

Written by African American composer James Bland (1854–1911), the tune has been the offical state song of Virginia since 1940.

Manuscripts, Archives, and Rare Books

BOX 808022   PETALUMA   CA 94975

LEST WE FORGET
The Triumph Over Slavery

Portrait of Men

Albumen print, c. 1865

Photographer: Attributed to G. Leuzinger

Photographs and Prints

BOX 808022   PETALUMA   CA 94975

Pomegranate

LEST WE FORGET
The Triumph Over Slavery

Colored National Convention

Wood engraving, 1876

Artist: C. C. Giers

Held in Nashville, Tennessee on April 5–7 and May 6, 1876,
delegates discussed the social, economic, and political future of
African Americans.

Photographs and Prints

BOX 808022   PETALUMA   CA 94975

Pomegranate

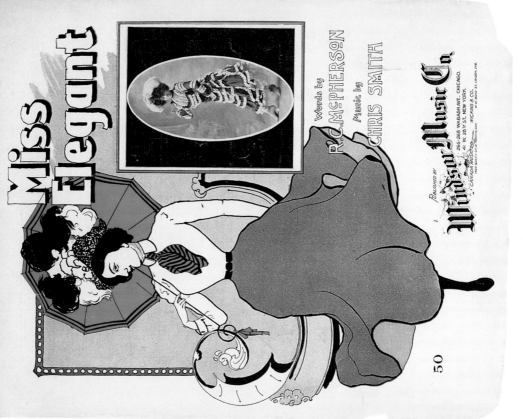

LEST WE FORGET
The Triumph Over Slavery

"Miss Elegant"

Sheet music cover, c. 1920s

From 1900 to 1924, R. C. McPherson wrote lyrics to many popular songs and eventually headed New York's first African American music publishing company.

Manuscripts, Archives, and Rare Books

BOX 808022   PETALUMA   CA 94975

LEST WE FORGET
The Triumph Over Slavery

First African Baptist Church of Savannah

Engraving, c. 1852

Founded on January 20, 1788, the Savannah church was one of the first black churches in North America. Its first pastor was Andrew Bryan, a slave.

Photographs and Prints

BOX 808022   PETALUMA   CA 94975

COME AND JOIN US BROTHERS.

PUBLISHED BY THE SUPERVISORY COMMITTEE FOR RECRUITING COLORED REGIMENTS

1210 CHESTNUT ST. PHILADELPHIA.

LEST WE FORGET
The Triumph Over Slavery

Come and Join Us Brothers

Union recruitment poster, 1863

Photographs and Prints

BOX 808022   PETALUMA   CA 94975

Pomegranate

AUCTION

107 YEARS OF PROGRESS

Having sold my farm and am leaving for Oregon territory by ox team, I will offer at public sale at my home 2 Miles South of Versailles, Kentucky, on McConn Ferry Pike, on

MARCH 1st, 1849

all my personal property, to wit:

ALL MY OX TEAMS

EXCEPT TWO TEAMS — BUCK and BEN, and TOM and JERRY

2 Milk Cows, one Gray Mare and Colt, 1 pair of oxen and yoke, one baby yoke, two ox carts, 1500 feet of poplar weather boards, plow with wooden moldboards, 800 to 1000 feet of clapboards, 1,000 ten-foot fence rails, one 60-gallon soap kettle, 85 sugar troughs, made of white ash timber; ten gallons of maple syrup; two spinning wheels; 30 pounds of mutton tallow; one large loom, made by Jerry Wilson; 300 poles; 100 split hoops, 100 empty barrels; one 32-gallon barrel of Johnson-Miller whiskey, 7 years old; 20 gallons of apple brandy; 40-gal. copper still; 1 doz. real books; two handle hooks; 3 scythes and cradles, 1 dozen wooden spiles; bullet mold and powder horm; rifle made by Ben Miller; 50 gallons of soft soap; hams, bacon, lard; 40 gallons of sorghum molasses.

SIX HEAD OF FOX HOUNDS   All Soft Mouthed

At the Same Time I Will Sell My   Except One

6 NEGRO SLAVES

Two men 35 years and 50 years old; two boys, 12 and 18 years old; two mulato wenches, 40 and 30 years old. We will sell all together to same party but will not separate them.

TERMS OF SALE — Cash in hand or note to draw 4 per cent interest with Bob McConnell as security.

PLENTY TO DRINK AND EAT

LEST WE FORGET
The Triumph Over Slavery

Slave Auction Broadside, c. 1850

Sample Noel Pittman Collection

BOX 808022   PETALUMA   CA 94975

Pomegranate

LEST WE FORGET
The Triumph Over Slavery

The Workers

Watercolor, 1993

Artist: Charles Lilly

Art and Artifacts

BOX 808022 PETALUMA CA 94975

Pomegranate

LEST WE FORGET
The Triumph Over Slavery

Returning from the Cotton Field in South Carolina

Stereographic image, c. 1870

Photographer: G.N. Barnard

Photographs and Prints

BOX 808022 PETALUMA CA 94975

Pomegranate

Death of Capt. Ferrer, the Captain of the Amistad, July, 1839.

Don Jose Ruiz and Don Pedro Montez, of the Island of Cuba, having purchased fifty-three slaves at Havana, recently imported from Africa, put them on board the Amistad, Capt. Ferrer, in order to transport them to Principe, another port on the Island of Cuba. After being out from Havana about four days, the African captives on board, in order to obtain their freedom, and return to Africa, armed themselves with cane knives, and rose upon the Captain and crew of the vessel. Capt. Ferrer and the cook of the vessel were killed; two of the crew escaped; Ruiz and Montez were made prisoners.

LEST WE FORGET
The Triumph Over Slavery

Death of Captain Ferrer, The Captain of the Amistad, *July, 1839*

Lithograph from *A History of the Amistad Captives,* 1840

Captured Africans frequently revolted on slave ships. Although shackles, chains, and guns were used to constrain them, they sometimes succeeded in overpowering their captors.

Manuscripts, Archives, and Rare Books

BOX 808022 PETALUMA CA 94975

Pomegranate

LEST WE FORGET
The Triumph Over Slavery

Storming Fort Wagner

Lithograph, 1890

Charge of the 54th Massachusetts Colored Regiment, July 18, 1863

Art and Artifacts

BOX 808022   PETALUMA   CA 94975

Pomegranate

MINUTES

AND

PROCEEDINGS

OF THE

FIRST ANNUAL CONVENTION

OF THE

PEOPLE OF COLOUR,

HELD BY ADJOURNMENTS IN THE

CITY OF PHILADELPHIA,

FROM THE

Sixth to the Eleventh of June,

INCLUSIVE,

1831.

PHILADELPHIA:

PUBLISHED BY ORDER OF THE COMMITTEE OF ARRANGEMENTS.

1831

LEST WE FORGET
The Triumph Over Slavery

Minutes and Proceedings of the First National Convention of the People of Color

Published in the *Salem Gazette,* November 8, 1831

Manuscripts, Archives, and Rare Books

BOX 808022   PETALUMA   CA 94975

Pomegranate

CELEBRATION OF FIFTEENTH AMENDMENT MAY 19TH 1870

LEST WE FORGET
The Triumph Over Slavery

The Fifteenth Amendment, 1869

Ratified by Congress on February 3, 1870, this amendment forbids the
federal government and the states from denying a citizen the right to
vote based on race, color, or previous status as a slave.

Art and Artifacts

BOX 808022   PETALUMA   CA 94975

LEST WE FORGET
The Triumph Over Slavery

African Burial Ground

Watercolor, 1994

Artist: Charles Lilly

More than 20,000 enslaved African men, women, and children were buried at the colonial-era African burial ground in lower Manhattan. Unearthed during construction of a federal office building in 1991, the cemetery covered more than five acres.

Charles Lilly Collection

BOX 808022   PETALUMA   CA 94975

Pomegranate

Benjamin Bannicker's
PENNSYLVANIA, DELAWARE, MARYLAND and VIRGINIA

Almanack

AND

EPHEMERIS,

FOR THE YEAR OF OUR LORD, 1 7 9 2;

Being BISSEXTILE, or LEAP-YEAR, and the SIX-TEENTH YEAR of AMERICAN INDEPENDENCE, which commenced *July 4, 1776.*

CONTAINING, the Motions of the Sun and Moon, the true Places and Aspects of the Planets, the Rising and Setting of the Sun, and the Rising, Setting and Southing, Place and Age of the Moon, &c.—The Lunations, Conjunctions, Eclipses, Judgment of the Weather, Festivals, and other remarkable Days; Days for holding the Supreme and Circuit Courts of the *United States*, as also the usual Courts in *Pennsylvania, Delaware, Maryland,* and *Virginia.*—Also, several useful Tables, and valuable Receipts.—Various Selections from the Commonplace-Book of the *Kentucky Philosopher*, an *American Sage*; with interesting and entertaining Essays, in Prose and Verse—the whole comprising a greater, more pleasing, and useful Variety, than any Work of the *Kind* and *Price* in *North-America.*

BALTIMORE: Printed and Sold, Wholesale and Retail, by WILLIAM GODDARD and JAMES ANGELL, at their Printing-Office, in *Market-Street.*—Sold, also, by Mr. JOSEPH CRUKSHANK, Printer, in *Market-Street,* and Mr. DANIEL HUMPHREYS, Printer, in *South-Front-Street, Philadelphia* and by Messrs. HANSON and BOND, Printers, in *Alexandria.*

LEST WE FORGET
The Triumph Over Slavery

Benjamin Bannicker's Almanack, c. 1792

Broadside for the first edition of the almanac published by Bannicker
(now usually spelled Banneker), a self-taught mathematician and
astronomer born in Baltimore County, Maryland, the son of freed slaves.

Manuscripts, Archives, and Rare Books

BOX 808022 PETALUMA CA 94975

MOLINEAUX.

Pub. by Dighton Spring Gardens Feb. 1. 1812.

LEST WE FORGET
The Triumph Over Slavery

Tom Molineaux

Etching, 1810

Artist: Robert Dighton

Born a slave, Molineaux (1784–1818) won his freedom and $100 by defeating a slave from a neighboring plantation in a boxing match. He traveled to London, becoming the first American to fight in an international bout. Although he lost two matches against British champion Tom Cribbs at the peak of his career, Molineaux holds the distinction of being America's first great boxer.

Manuscripts, Archives, and Rare Books

BOX 808022   PETALUMA   CA 94975

Pomegranate

LEST WE FORGET
The Triumph Over Slavery

Market Woman

Albumen print, c. 1870

Photographer: Alberto Henschel

Photographs and Prints

Pomegranate

BOX 808022   PETALUMA   CA 94975

LEST WE FORGET
The Triumph Over Slavery

Portrait of a Man with Scarification

Albumen print, c. 1880

Photographer: Rodolpho Lindemann

Photographs and Prints

BOX 808022   PETALUMA   CA 94975

Pomegranate

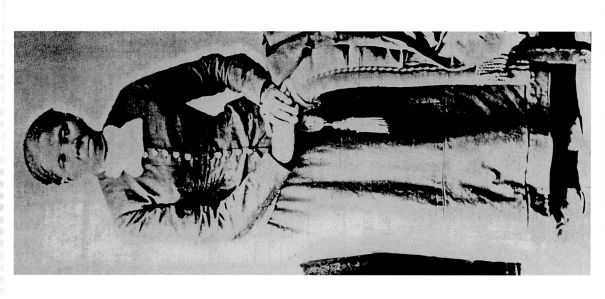

LEST WE FORGET
The Triumph Over Slavery

Harriet Tubman

Born a slave, Harriet Tubman (1820–1913) ran away from a Maryland plantation in 1849 and soon afterward began to help others escape. Feared by slaveholders, Tubman made some nineteen trips to and from the South to guide more than two hundred Underground Railroad "passengers" to freedom. Tubman lived with a $40,000 bounty on her life.

Photographs and Prints

CA 94975 PETALUMA BOX 808022

Published according to Act of Parliament, Sept.ʳ 1.1773 by Archᵈ Bell,
Bookseller Nᵒ 8 near the Saracens Head Aldgate.

P O E M S

ON

VARIOUS SUBJECTS,

RELIGIOUS AND MORAL.

BY

PHILLIS WHEATLEY,

NEGRO SERVANT to Mr. JOHN WHEATLEY,
of BOSTON, in NEW ENGLAND.

L O N D O N:

Printed for A. BELL, Bookseller, Aldgate; and sold b
Messrs. COX and BERRY, King-Street, BOSTON.

MDCCLXXIII.

LEST WE FORGET
The Triumph Over Slavery

Poems on Various Subjects, Religious and Moral, 1773

Author: Phyllis Wheatley

Born in Africa and enslaved in America, Phyllis Wheatley was the first published African American author.

Manuscripts, Archives, and Rare Books

BOX 808022   PETALUMA   CA 94975

Pomegranate

LEST WE FORGET
The Triumph Over Slavery

Negre & Négresse dans Une Plantation

Lithograph, c. 1835

Artist: Johann Mortiz Rugendas

Lithographer: Deroy

Published in *Voyage Pittoresque et Historique au Brésil, Paris*

Art and Artifacts

BOX 808022   PETALUMA   CA 94975

Pomegranate

LEST WE FORGET
The Triumph Over Slavery

Portrait of a Woman, Bahia, Brazil

Albumen print, c. 1880

Photographer: Rodolpho Lindemann

More than 3.5 million slaves were transported to Brazil during the slavery era, more than to any colony in the Americas.

Photographs and Prints

BOX 808022 PETALUMA CA 94975

ANGOLA.

MONJOLO.

BENGUELA.

CONGO.

LEST WE FORGET
The Triumph Over Slavery

Benguela/Angola/Congo/Monjolo

Lithograph, c. 1835

Artist: Johann Mortiz Rugendas

Lithographer: Pierre-Roch Vigneron

Published in *Voyage Pittoresque et Historique au Brésil,* Paris, c. 1835

Art and Artifacts

BOX 808022 PETALUMA CA 94975

LEST WE FORGET
The Triumph Over Slavery

Toussaint L'Ouverture Rec. Proclamation, 1821

The eldest son born to slaves, François-Dominique Toussaint
L'Overture (c. 1743–1803) became one of the founding fathers of Haiti
after taking inspiration from the philosophy of the Enlightenment—
liberty, equality, and fraternity—during the French Revolution.

Art and Artifacts

BOX 808022   PETALUMA   CA 94975

LEST WE FORGET
The Triumph Over Slavery

Ira Aldridge, 1853

Engraving, n.d.

Born to a free black family in New York City in 1807, Ira Aldridge
received his education at the African Free School on Mulberry Street.
By 1835 he was headlining as Othello in London and Dublin.

Photographs and Prints

BOX 808022   PETALUMA   CA 94975

Pomegranate

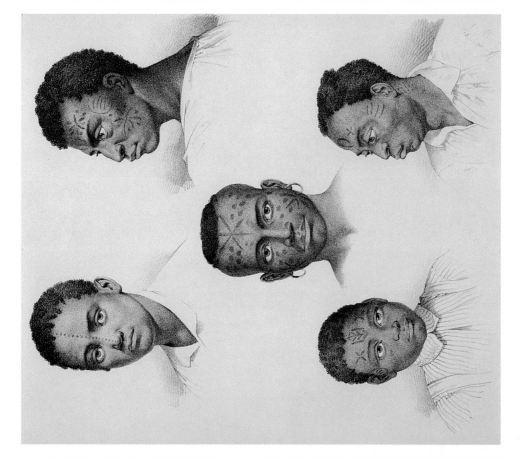

LEST WE FORGET
The Triumph Over Slavery

Mozambique

Lithograph, c. 1835
Artist: Johann Mortiz Rugendas
Lithographer: Pierre-Roch Vigneron
Published in *Voyage Pittoresque et Historique au Brésil,* Paris
Art and Artifacts

Pomegranate

BOX 808022   PETALUMA   CA 94975

LEST WE FORGET
The Triumph Over Slavery

Booker T. Washington, 1911

Booker Taliaferro Washington (1856–1915) was freed from slavery as a nine-year-old. At sixteen, he attended Hampton Normal and Agricultural Institute to become a teacher, and later was the first leader of the Tuskegee Institute in 1881. Washington achieved national prominence for his Atlanta Address of 1895. He helped raise funds to establish and operate hundreds of schools and institutions of higher education while working to improve racial relations in the United States.

Photographs and Prints

BOX 808022   PETALUMA   CA 94975

Pomegranate

LEST WE FORGET
The Triumph Over Slavery

Sojourner Truth

Born Isabella Baumfree, Truth (1797–1883) changed her name after escaping slavery. Inspired by a spiritual revelation, she preached "God's truth and plan for salvation." Later, she worked with abolitionists, including Frederick Douglass, and also labored for women's suffrage. At an 1851 convention in Akron, Ohio, Truth posed the legendary question, "Ain't I a woman?" After the Civil War, she aided newly freed southern slaves. Her memoir, *The Narrative of Sojourner Truth: A Northern Slave,* was published in 1850.

Photographs and Prints

BOX 808022   PETALUMA   CA 94975

HEROES OF THE COLORED RACE.

LEST WE FORGET
The Triumph Over Slavery

Heroes of the Colored Race

Lithograph, 1881

Artist: J. Hoover

Most prominently featured on the poster are Blanche K. Bruce, Frederick Douglass, and Hiram Revels.

Art and Artifacts

BOX 808022   PETALUMA   CA 94975

Pomegranate